ITALIAN RECIPE COOKBOOK:

DELICIOUS AND HEALTHY ITALIAN MEALS

CHEF PAOLO FERRARI

Introduction:

The Italian way of life is quite beautiful, offering long days of olive-eating, wine drinking, and pasta munching—all without that burdensome gut caused by the normal American diet.

This forces us to ask the question: what do the Italians know that we just don't?

Essentially, they know the value of quality foods.

Furthermore, however, the Italian, Mediterranean-based diet offers many health benefits. It works to refute heart disease, many cancers, and boost the length for life.

Look to the following tips to better understand the beautiful way to Dine Like an Italian, today!

1. Italians only eat until they're full.

That's right: unlike the American way of life, the Italians actually stop eating when they fill their tummies. They get the signal, and then they place their fork down. It's as simple as that!

2. Italians dine slowly, throughout many hours.

You won't see many Italians scarfing their pasta down their throats quickly, like many Americans. Rather, they eat casually throughout many hours, enjoying wine, conversation, and people watching.

3. Italians enjoy simplistic ingredients.

The recipes in this book are backed with tomatoes, with zucchinis, with olives, and with pasta. No crazy ingredients are found here. Rather, the Italians look to simple, fresh ingredients for their health and wellness.

The healthy, vibrant foods included in this book help you recognize when you're full because they fill you with healthful fiber. Furthermore, they work to refute dangerous diseases, like cancers, because of their anti-inflammatory properties.

Of course, the Italians always have time to laugh, to enjoy life, as well. They turn toward their Tiramisu's as much as the next person. But perhaps they only have a bit (or three).

Enjoy the healthy, Italian appetizers, salads, soups, pizzas, pastas, and desserts in this book. You won't regret sitting down for a long, luxurious, and filling meal.

After all: this food is good for the soul.

TABLE OF CONTENTS

.

Chapter 1. Italian Appetizer Recipes

Prosciutto and Ricotta Bites

Recipe Makes 12 Bites.

Nutritional Information Per Serving: 105 calories, 1 gram carbohydrates, 7 grams fat, 5 grams protein.

Ingredients:

1 ¼ cup ricotta cheese

4 minced garlic cloves

1/3 cup sliced prosciutto

1 ½ cup diced spinach

Directions:

Preheat the oven to 350 degrees Fahrenheit.

Next, stir together the spinach, the garlic, and the ricotta. Set this mixture to the side.

Next, align the prosciutto at the bottom of a mini muffin tin. They should line the bottom and come up over the tops.

Fill the mini muffin tins with the cheese mixture.

Bake the bites for fifteen minutes. The prosciutto should be brown.

Serve the bites warm, and enjoy!

CLASSIC ANTIPASTO WITH ARTICHOKES AND PROVOLONE CHEESE

Recipe Makes 8 Servings.

Nutritional Information Per Serving: 430 calories, 15 grams carbohydrates, 32 grams fat, 17 grams protein.

Ingredients:

18 ounces artichoke hearts

12 ounces diced red peppers

1 ¼ pound diced provolone cheese

15 ounces black olives

½ cup olive oil

1 tsp. dried oregano

1/3 cup balsamic vinegar

½ tsp. salt

½ tsp. pepper

10 sliced basil leaves

Directions:

Dump the artichoke hearts into a large container. Add the olives, the provolone, and the peppers. Stir.

Next, to the side, stir together the vinegar, the olive oil, the salt, the pepper, and the oregano. Pour this mixture over the artichoke mixture, and seal the container.

Refrigerate the mixture for three hours. Make sure to stir it every one hour throughout.

Serve the salad at room temperature with the basil overtop.

Enjoy!

Parmesan Bruschetta

Recipe Makes 6 Servings.

Nutritional Breakdown Per Serving: 175 calories, 22 grams carbohydrates, 7 grams fat, 5 grams protein.

Ingredients:

1 pound sliced Italian bread

2 diced tomatoes

1 diced onion

2 tbsp. olive oil

½ tbsp. diced oregano

2 tsp. diced parsley

1 tsp. diced basil

1/3 cup grated Parmesan cheese

Directions:

Preheat the oven to 425 degrees Fahrenheit.

To the side, stir together the olive oil, the tomatoes, the onion, and the spices.

Place the sliced bread on a baking sheet. Add the tomato mixture, and then add a layer of Parmesan over the tomato.

Bake the bread for ten minutes. Allow the bread to cool, and then serve.

Enjoy!

MEDITERRANEAN OLIVE DIP

Recipe Makes 8 Servings.

Nutritional Information Per Serving: 50 calories, 2 grams carbohydrates, 7 grams fat, 1 gram protein.

Ingredients:

1 ¼ cup black olives

4 minced garlic cloves

3 tbsp. lemon juice

2 tbsp. capers

4 tbsp. diced parsley

2 tbsp. olive oil

½ tsp. salt

½ tsp. pepper

Directions:

Bring all the above ingredients into a food processor.

Puree the ingredients until smooth. Serve with crackers, and enjoy!

Chapter 2: Italian Salad Recipes

Italian Mid-Day Panzanella Bread Salad

Recipe Makes 10 Servings.

Nutritional Information Per Serving: 260 calories, 25 grams carbohydrates, 15 gams fat, 8 grams protein.

Ingredients:

10 ounces diced white bread

12 halved olives

4 tbsp. olive oil

2 cups halved cherry tomatoes

15 ounces garbanzo beans

½ up diced red pepper

1 diced onion

1/3 cup balsamic vinegar

1/3 cup pest

6 ounces crumbled goat cheese

1/3 cup toasted pine nuts

1 head green lettuce

Directions:

Begin by preheating the oven to 350 degrees Fahrenheit.

Next, place the bread and the olive oil in a bowl and toss. Add salt and toss once more.

Place the bread on a baking sheet and bake them for thirteen minutes. Allow them to cool.

Next, mix together the beans, the peppers, the tomatoes, the onions, and the kalamata olives in a big serving bowl.

To the side, stir together the spices, the pesto, and the vinegar. Pour this over the vegetables mixture and toss well. Allow it to sit in your kitchen—not in the fridge—for one hour.

Add the bread and the goat cheese to the salad and toss well. Serve the salad over the lettuce leaves, and enjoy with the pine nuts overtop.

Italian Garlic Eggplant Salad

Recipe Makes 12 Servings.

Nutritional Information Per Serving: 100 calories, 15 grams carbohydrates, 3 grams fat, 2 grams protein.

Ingredients:

7 eggplants

3 minced garlic cloves

4 tbsp. olive oil

1 tbsp. balsamic vinegar

4 tbsp. olive oil

1 tbsp. sugar

½ tsp. basil

½ tsp. oregano

½ tsp. salt

½ tsp. pepper

Directions:

Preheat the oven to 350 degrees Fahrenheit. Pierce each of the full eggplants with a knife and place them on a baking sheet. Bake them for ninety minutes, making sure to turn them every thirty minutes.

Allow the eggplants to cool. Peel them and dice them into small pieces.

To the side, stir together all the ingredients, including the diced eggplant. Place the salad in the refrigerator and allow it to marinate for three hours.

Serve, and enjoy!

Picnic Italian Pasta Salad

Recipe Makes 8 Servings.

Nutritional Information Per Serving: 230 calories, 26 grams carbohydrates, 12 grams fat, 6 grams protein.

Ingredients:

10 ounces spiral pasta, pre-cooked

1 cup diced broccoli

1 cup diced green peppers

1 cup diced mushrooms

½ cup sliced olives

1/3 cup cubed Mozzarella cheese

1 cup Italian dressing

Directions:

Bring all the ingredients together into a large bowl, and toss well to coat.

Enjoy!

Pepperoni Italian Salad

Recipe Makes 8 Servings.

Nutritional Information Per Serving: 333 calories, 6 grams carbohydrates, 30 grams fat, 18 grams protein.

Ingredients:

8 cups shredded lettuce

1 cup diced yellow pepper

1 cup halved grape tomatoes

2 cups cubed mozzarella cheese

1 ¼ cup diced fennel bulb

10 ounce pepperoni, diced

1 cup sour cream

½ cup mayonnaise

1/3 cup milk

½ tsp. salt

1 tsp. dried basil

½ tsp. pepper

Directions:

Layer the salad in a large salad bowl. First, position the lettuce at the bottom. Next, add the bell peppers, the tomatoes, the fennel, the cheese, and the pepperoni.

Next, mix together all the ingredients from the sour cream to the pepper. Pour this dressing over the vegetables, and allow the salad to chill for three hours.

Enjoy!

Chapter 3: Italian Soup Recipes

Italian Vineyard Wedding Soup

Recipe Makes 4 Servings.

Nutritional Information Per Serving: 430 calories, 47 grams carbohydrates, 28 grams protein, 14 grams fat.

Ingredients:

¾ pound ground beef

1 egg

3 tbsp. dried bread crumbs

2 tbsp. Parmesan cheese

6 cups chicken broth

½ tsp. onion powder

2 cups sliced escarole

½ tsp. dried basil

1 ¼ cup orzo pasta, dry

½ cup diced carrots

Directions:

Stir together the cheese, the spices, the meat, the egg, and the bread crumbs. With your fingers, shape the mixture into small, one-inch meatballs.

To the side, heat the broth to boiling. Add the orzo, the escarole, the meatballs, and the carrot. Allow the water to begin to boil once more. Reduce the heat to medium at this time.

Cook the soup for twelve additional minutes at a simmer. The pasta should be al dente.

Enjoy!

ITALIAN FROM THE GARDEN ONION SOUP

Recipe Makes 4 Servings.

Nutritional Information Per Serving: 350 calories, 44 grams carbohydrates, 12 grams fat, 13 grams protein.

Ingredients:

1 tbsp. diced garlic

2 tbsp. olive oil

1/3 cup balsamic vinegar

10 cups sliced onion

½ tsp. salt

½ tsp. dried sage

32 ounces beef broth

4 slices Italian bread

1 ¼ cup shredded mozzarella cheese

Directions:

Heat the olive oil in a large skillet over medium.

Add the garlic and cook until the garlic browns.

Add the onion and the salt and cook for eight minutes.

Reduce the heat to medium, and cook for ten minutes more, stirring all the time. The onions should be golden.

Next, add the vinegar and the dried sage. Cook for five minutes, until the liquid evaporates.

At this time, add the broth.

Allow the mixture to simmer for twelve minutes, stirring every few moments.

At this time, set the oven to broil.

Add the cheese over the bread, and place the bread on the baking sheet.

Broil the pieces of bread about five inches from the heat. The cheese should be melted.

Serve the soup with the bread, and enjoy!

Zucchini Italian Soup

Recipe Makes 10 Servings.

Nutritional Information Per Serving: 110 calories, 24 grams carbohydrates, 1 gram fat, 4 grams protein.

Ingredients:

10 cups sliced zucchini

10 ounces canned tomato soup

7 cups diced tomatoes

2 ¼ cup sliced green peppers

3 cups diced celery

4 tbsp. sugar

2 cups diced onion

2 tsp. salt

1 tsp. pepper

Directions:

Stir together the vegetables, the sugar, the tomato soup, the salt, and the pepper in a large soup pot. Stir and allow it to come to a boil.

At this time, reduce the heat to low. Allow the mixture to simmer for forty minutes.

The zucchini should be tender.

Serve warm, and enjoy!

Italian Tortellini Soup

Recipe Makes 6 Servings.

Nutritional Information Per Serving: 250 calories, 25 grams carbohydrates, 8 grams fat, 12 grams protein.

Ingredients:

4 ounces Italian sausage, removed from casing

1 diced onion

3 minced garlic cloves

1 tsp. dried basil

6 cups beef broth

1 diced zucchini

1 cup tomato sauce

½ cup red wine

½ cup water

5 sliced tomatoes

1 cup diced carrots

10 ounces cheese tortellini

1 tbsp. chopped, fresh parsley

2 tbsp. grated Parmesan cheese

Directions:

Cook the sausage in a big soup pot over medium-high heat. Saute for twelve minutes. It should be browned.

Drain the fat, keeping only a tbsp.

At this time, add the onion and the garlic. Saute for six minutes more.

Next, add the beef broth, the wine, the water, the carrots, the tomatoes, the oregano, the basil, and the tomato sauce. Bring the mixture to a boil, and then reduce the heat to low.

At this time, allow the soup to simmer for thirty minutes. Remove all fat that appears at the surface, and discard.

Add the tortellini, the green pepper, the parsley, and the zucchini at this time. Simmer for an additional twelve minutes. The tortellini should be fully cooked.

Serve the soup warm and add the grated Parmesan cheese.

Enjoy!

Italian Chowder

Recipe Makes 8 Servings.

Nutritional Information Per Serving: 260 calories, 10 grams carbohydrates, 10 grams fat, 31 grams protein.

Ingredients:

3 pounds cubed halibut

1 diced onion

1 diced red pepper

2 diced celery stalks

4 minced garlic cloves

1/3 cup olive oil

1 cup tomato juice

32 ounces diced tomatoes

3 tbsp. diced, fresh parsley

1/3 cup apple juice

½ tsp. dried thyme

½ tsp. salt

½ tsp. pepper

Directions:

Saute all the vegetables and the garlic in the olive oil in a large soup pot for six minutes.

At this time, add the tomato juice, the apple juice, the diced tomato, and all the herbs.

Simmer the soup for thirty-five minutes on medium-low.

Add the halibut at this time. Cook for thirty minutes.

Salt and pepper the soup, and serve warm.

Enjoy!

Chapter 4: Italian Pizza Recipes

Vibrant Pesto Mediterranean Pizza

Recipe Makes 1 pizza, 8 slices.

Nutritional Information Per Serving: 270 calories, 18 grams carbohydrates, 15 grams fat, 12 grams protein.

Ingredients:

10 ounces refrigerated pizza dough

1/3 cup diced fresh parsley

8 ounces sliced mozzarella cheese

1/3 cup pesto

½ cup prosciutto

4 tbsp. diced fresh basil

4 tbsp. grated Parmesan cheese

Directions:

Preheat the oven to 400 degrees Fahrenheit.

Next, roll the pizza dough out on a large oven stone.

Add the pesto like sauce over the crust.

Add the mozzarella over the pesto. Next, add the prosciutto.

Add the basil, the parsley, and the Parmesan at this time.

Bake the pizza for eleven minutes in the preheated oven, making sure the crust is browned and the cheese is melted and delicious.

Enjoy!

Easter Sunday Italian Pizza

Recipe Makes 24 Servings.

Nutritional Information Per Serving: 400 calories, 25 grams carbohydrates, 24 grams fat, 21 grams protein.

Ingredients:

5 ½ cups flour

3 ½ pounds diced Italian sausage

½ tsp. salt

1 tsp. sugar

16 ounces ricotta cheese

8 uncooked eggs

9 hard boiled eggs, sliced in half

1 tbsp. baking powder

1/3 cup olive oil

1 cup milk

1 tsp. pepper

Directions:

Stir together the flour, the sugar, the salt, and the baking powder in a large bowl.

To the side, mix together the milk, the oil, and 3 of the eggs. Pour this mixture into the dry mixture, and stir until the dough is sticky.

Preheat the oven to 350 degrees Fahrenheit at this time.

Split the dough into two pieces. Roll out one of the halves and lay it in an 18x14 inch baking sheet. The sides should come up about a half an inch. Pin the dough to each of the sides, and set the dough to the side.

Cook the sausage in a big skillet over medium heat, stirring until it's no longer pink. Discard of the grease, and set the sausage to the side.

When the sausage cools, mix it with 5 eggs, the ricotta cheese, the pepper, and all the hard boiled eggs in a big mixing bowl.

Spread the above mixture over the dough in the baking pan.

To the side, roll out the rest of the dough and spread it over the top. Pinch the edges together to make a seal.

Bake the Easter pizza in the oven for sixty minutes. Allow it to cool for fifteen minutes before slicing.

Enjoy!

Deep Dish Pizza Lover's Alfredo Sauce Pizza

Recipe Makes 8 Servings.

Nutritional Information Per Serving: 440 calories, 26 grams carbohydrates, 37 grams fat, 13 grams protein.

Ingredients:

1 cup water

1/3 cup butter

1/3 cup olive oil

¼ ounce active yeast

1 ¾ cups flour

2 tbsp. cream cheese

1 cup grated Parmesan

1 tsp. garlic powder

2 cups mozzarella cheese

Directions:

To the side, stir together the oil, the water, and the yeast. Add the flour.

Roll the mixture into a ball and place it in a bowl that has been oiled. Allow the crust to rise for one hour in a warm room. It should double in its size.

Punch the dough immediately after and place it in a deep-dish pizza pan.

Cover the dough with a cloth. Let the crust rise an additional twenty-five minutes more, until it's puffy.

Preheat the oven to 450 degrees Fahrenheit.

Next, stir together the butter, the cream, ad the cream cheese. Pour it into a saucepan and heat over medium, stirring all the time until melted.

Add the Parmesan cheese and the garlic powder at this time. Cook and stir for the following eighteen minutes, until the Parmesan cheese looks golden.

Spread this mixture over the pizza, and then top the pizza with Mozzarella cheese

Bake the pizza in the oven for thirty-five minutes. Allow it to cool for a moment before slicing and enjoying!

Best Margherita Pizza

Recipe Makes 4 Servings.

Nutritional Information Per Serving: 350 calories, 35 grams carbohydrates, 20 grams fat, 10 grams protein.

Ingredients:

1 ½ cups flour

¼ ounce rapid rise yeast

1 tsp. salt

2 tsp. sugar

½ cup water

4 tbsp. olive oil, separated

2 tsp. minced garlic

2 sliced tomatoes

½ tsp. pepper

½ tsp. salt

1 ½ cup shredded Italian cheese

1 tsp. herb seasoning of your choice

Directions:

Preheat the oven to 425 degrees Fahrenheit.

Next, mix together half of the flour, the sugar, the yeast, and the salt. Stir, and then add the warm water and half of the olive oil.

Stir the mixture until it's well blended. This should take about one minute.

Next, add the remaining flour and form the mixture into a soft dough. The dough should be a ball. Knead it on a surface, placing flour beneath so as not to loose any dough.

Knead the dough for about five minutes. At this time, allow the dough to sit for ten minutes.

After ten minutes, fill a pizza pan with the dough.

To the side, stir together the other half of the olive oil and the garlic. Slather it over the dough.

Add the salt, the tomato, and the basil. Sprinkle cheese overtop. Add herb seasoning.

Bake the pizza for about fifteen minutes. The cheese should be bubbling, and the crust should be golden brown.

Enjoy!

Spaghetti Delight Pizza

Recipe Makes 7 Servings.

Nutritional Information Per Serving: 350 calories, 34 grams carbohydrates, 15 grams fat, 18 grams protein.

Ingredients:

10 ounces spaghetti, broken into small pieces

1/3 cup milk

1 egg

½ tsp. salt

2 ½ cups shredded mozzarella

15 ounces spaghetti sauce

½ tsp. dried basil

½ tsp. dried oregano

5 ounces sliced sausage

Preheat the oven to 425 degrees Fahrenheit.

Next, allow a large pot of water to boil. Cook the spaghetti in the boiling water for ten minutes. Drain and rinse the noodles in cold water.

Next, mix together the milk, the eggs, one half of the mozzarella cheese, the garlic, and the salt in a big mixing bowl. Add the cooked spaghetti and stir well.

Next, spread this mixture at the bottom of a 9x13 baking dish. Bake the mixture for fifteen minutes.

At this time, reduce the heat of your oven to 350 degrees Fahrenheit.

Next, spread the sauce over the noodles. Add the oregano, the rest of the mozzarella, and the basil. Add the pepperoni, as well.

Return the pizza to the oven. Bake for an additional thirty minutes. The cheese should be bubbly and a bit brown.

Remove the pizza from the oven and allow it to sit for five minutes before diving into it.

Enjoy!

Chapter 5: Italian Main Dish Recipes

Simple Italian Sausage Pasta

Recipe Makes 6 Servings.

Nutritional Information Per Serving: 340 calories, 30 grams carbohydrates, 20 grams fat, 15 grams protein.

Ingredients:

1 pound Italian sausage

8 ounces tomato sauce

1 ½ cups water

14 ounces diced tomatoes

10 ounces dried penne pasta

1/3 cup grated Parmesan cheese

Directions:

Heat a skillet over medium. Cook the sausage for five minutes, breaking it in order to crumble it. When it browns, drain the grease.

Add the water, the tomatoes, the tomato sauce, and the penne pasta. Stir well and bring the mixture to a boil.

Cover the mixture and reduce the heat to low. Cook the mixture for about fifteen minutes. The pasta should be tender.

Add Parmesan cheese. Stir well, and serve warm.

Enjoy!

Vineyard Italian Lasagna

Recipe Makes 16 Servings.

Nutritional Information Per Serving: 600 calories, 30 grams carbohydrates, 40 grams fat, 35 grams protein.

Ingredients:

10 slices diced pre-cooked bacon

2 pints ricotta cheese

1 diced onion

2 eggs

1 tsp. fennel seeds

2 tsp. Italian seasoning

1 tsp. oregano

3 tsp. fresh parsley

½ cup milk

56 ounces tomato sauce

1 ¾ pound Italian sausage

10 slices provolone cheese

5 cups mozzarella cheese, shredded

16 ounces lasagna noodles

Directions:

Cook the bacon and the onion together in a large skillet over medium.

Add the oregano, the fennel, the seasoning, and the tomato sauce. Cover the mixture and allow it to simmer on LOW for six hours. It should thicken.

After six hours, preheat the oven to 350 degrees Fahrenheit.

Next, brown the sausage in a big skillet.

After the meat is browned, drain the skillet and then slice the sausage into bite-sized pieces.

Mix the egg, the ricotta, and the milk in a medium-sized bowl.

Next, slather 1 cup of the prepared sauce in the bottom of a 9x13 pan.

Add 1/3 of the lasagna noodles.

Add half of the ricotta cheese.

Add ½ of the sausage.

Add 1/3 of the mozzarella.

Add ½ of the provolone cheese.

Add 1/3 of the prepared sauce.

Repeat these layers until you run out, and then spread the sauce over top.

Sprinkle the last of the mozzarella cheese over the sauce, and bake the lasagna for ninety minutes in the preheated oven.

Enjoy!

ITALIAN RIGATONI

Recipe Makes 12 Servings.

Nutritional Information Per Serving: 375 calories, 35 grams carbohydrates, 17 grams fat, 15 grams protein.

Ingredients:

20 ounces Italian sausage links

1 diced red pepper

4 tbsp. olive oil

16 ounces pre-cooked rigatoni pasta noodles

3 minced garlic cloves

25 ounces marinara sauce

3 tbsp. Italian parsley

Directions:

Cook the sausage in a large skillet. When they're cooked thoroughly, drain the grease and slice them into small, bite-sized pieces.

Next, heat the oil in the same skillet. Saute the pepper and the garlic for five minutes.

At this time, add the sausage, the marinara sauce, and the pasta. Cook until completely heated.

Add the parsley and stir. Serve warm, and enjoy!

Italian Chicken Parmesan

Recipe Makes 6 Servings.

Nutritional Information Per Serving: 500 calories, 31 grams carbohydrates, 22 grams fat, 44 grams protein.

Ingredients:

2 eggs

1 cup grated Parmesan

1 tbsp. olive oil

8 ounces bread crumbs

3 boneless and skinless chicken breasts, sliced in half

10 ounces pasta sauce of your choice

6 slices Provolone Cheese

Directions:

Preheat the oven to 375 degrees Fahrenheit.

Beat the eggs in the bottom of a small bowl.

In another dish, mix together the Parmesan and the bread crumbs.

First, dip the chicken into the egg. Then, dip it into the bread crumbs. Make sure you fully coat the chicken.

To the side, heat the olive oil over medium heat in a large skillet. Place the chicken in the skillet and sauté the chicken for ten minutes on each of its sides. The chicken should be completely cooked, all the way through.

Pour the tomato sauce into the bottom of a 9x13 pan. Place the chicken in the baking dish and place a piece of cheese over each piece of chicken.

Bake the chicken in the preheated oven for twenty minutes. The cheese should be melted.

Enjoy!

Italian-Inspired Meatloaf

Recipe Makes 8 Servings.

Nutritional Information Per Serving: 295 calories, 23 grams carbohydrates, 13 grams fat, 20 grams protein.

Ingredients:

¾ cup sun-dried tomatoes

1 cup diced fresh basil

1 cup water

1/3 cup ketchup

¼ cup tomato sauce

3 ounces shredded provolone cheese

3 minced garlic cloves

2 egg whites

1 ¼ cup bread crumbs

1 ¼ pound ground beef

1 cup diced onion

Directions:

Place the tomatoes in the bottom of a bowl. Pour the water over the tomatoes and soak them for forty-five minutes. At this time, drain the water.

Next, preheat the oven to 350 degrees Fahrenheit.

Stir together the tomatoes, the beef, the onion, the crumbs, the basil, the provolone, the sauce, the ketchup, the egg whites, and the garlic together in a large bowl.

Pack the mixture into a bread pan.

Bake the meatloaf for sixty minutes. If you utilize a meat thermometer, the inside of the meat should read 160 degrees Fahrenheit.

Allow the meatloaf to cool for a moment, and then slice.

Serve and enjoy!

Italian Artichoke and Salami Frittata

Recipe Makes 6 Servings.

Nutritional Information Per Serving: 211 calories, 5 grams carbohydrates, 13 grams fat, 17 grams protein.

Ingredients:

2 minced garlic cloves

1/3 cup diced salami

¾ cup diced cherry tomatoes

½ cup chopped artichoke hearts

6 eggs

5 ounces sliced mushrooms

3 diced green onions

1 cup shredded mozzarella

½ cup grated Parmesan cheese

½ tsp. salt

½ tsp. pepper

1 tsp. onion powder

Directions:

Preheat the oven to 425 degrees Fahrenheit.

Next, heat a skillet over medium. Cook the artichokes, the salami, the mushrooms, and the tomatoes for five minutes.

At this time, pour this mixture into an 8x8 baking dish.

To the side, stir together the milk, the eggs, the onions, the basil, the onion powder, and the salt and pepper. Pour this mixture over the salami and artichoke mixture.

Add the Parmesan and the mozzarella cheese over the eggs. Bake in the oven for twenty minutes.

Enjoy!

Italian Gnocchi

Recipe Makes 2 Servings.

Nutritional Information Per Serving: 450 calories, 91 grams carbohydrates, 3 grams fat, 15 grams protein.

Ingredients:

1 ¼ cup potato flakes, dried

1 tsp. salt

1 ¼ cup boiling water

½ tsp. pepper

1 egg

1 ¾ cup flour

Directions:

Place the potato flakes in a large mixing bowl. Pour the boiling water over the potato flakes and stir until completely mixed.

Allow the mixture to cool.

After it cools, add the salt, the egg, and the pepper. Add a bit of flour, stirring until you create a tough dough.

Place the dough on a floured board and knead at it.

Split the dough into two halves. Create two long, thin pieces. They should look sort of like breadsticks.

Slice the rolls into small, bite-sized gnocchi pieces.

Boil a large pot of water. Drop a few of the gnocchi into the water. When the gnocchi rise to the top, catch them with a spoon.

Repeat this process with all the gnocchi pieces. Allow them to cool, and serve with your favorite sauce!

Enjoy!

Butternut Squash Ravioli

Recipe Makes 6 Servings.

Nutritional Information Per Serving: 375 calories, 40 grams carbohydrates, 15 grams fat, 11 grams protein.

Ingredients:

1 ¼ cup mashed butternut squash

½ cup grated Parmesan cheese

16 ounces wonton wrappers

2 tbsp. butter

3/4 cup mascarpone cheese

2 garlic cloves

1 egg yolk

Directions:

After you've cooked the squash, place it in a mixing bowl and mash it with the pepper, the salt, the egg yolk, the mascarpone cheese, and the Parmesan cheese. Stir until completely smooth.

Next, position a wonton wrapper on a floured surface. Wet your finger in water and place it along the outside edge of the wonton wrapper in order to wet it lightly.

Place 1 tsp. of the filling in the middle of the wonton, and then fold the wonton in half. Press at the edges to seal.

Do this over and over again, until you've filled all the wonton wrappers.

Place a skillet over medium-high heat. Add the butter and the cloves of garlic. Heat.

To the side, allow a small saucepan of water to come to a boil.

Drop each of the raviolis into the water. Cook until they float up to the top. This should take about two minutes.

After this, drain the raviolis. Place them in the skillet.

Cook the raviolis until they're garlic-y. This should take about three minutes. Add any salt, pepper, and spices you like.

Enjoy!

Tortellini Bake Casserole

Recipe Makes 8 Servings.

Nutritional Information Per Serving: 400 calories, 30 grams carbohydrates, 20 grams fat, 20 grams protein.

Ingredients:

1 ¼ pound Italian sausage

14 ounces diced tomatoes

1 diced onion

1 diced green pepper

24 ounces marinara sauce

1 tsp. garlic powder

10 ounces tortellini, all filled with cheese

2 ½ cups mozzarella cheese, shredded

Directions:

Heat a saucepan over medium. Add the sausage, the onion, and the green pepper. Cook for about ten minutes, stirring occasionally. After ten minutes, discard the grease.

Add the marinara sauce at this time along with the diced tomatoes. Add the seasoning and stir.

Allow the mixture to come to a simmer. At this time, reduce the heat to medium-low and cook until the tomatoes break into the sauce. This should take about fifty minutes.

At this time, preheat the oven to 350 degrees Fahrenheit.

Allow a large pot of water to come to a boil. Cook the tortellini in the pot of water for about eight minutes. Drain.

Place the tortellini in the prepared sauce at this time. Cook for another six minutes.

Pour the mixture into the 9x13 baking dish. Add mozzarella cheese overtop and any salt and pepper you please.

Bake the casserole for twenty-five to thirty minutes. The cheese should be golden brown.

Allow the casserole to cool. Slice and serve. Enjoy!

Chapter 6: Italian Dessert Recipes

Italian Wedding Cookies

Recipe Makes 80 Cookies.

Nutritional Information Per Serving: 140 calories, 11 grams carbohydrates, 8 grams fat, 2 grams protein.

Ingredients:

1 ¼ cup butter

1 cup confectioners' sugar

5 tsp. vanilla

3 cups flour

1 tsp. salt

1 ¾ cups ground almonds

¼ cup (or more) extra confectioners' sugar for rolling

Directions:

Preheat the oven to 325 degrees Fahrenheit.

Next, cream the butter in a mixing bowl. Add the sugar and the salt gradually, and beat the butter until it's fluffy.

At this time, add the ground almonds and the vanilla. Continue to beat.

Next, shape the dough into small balls, utilizing about 1 tsp.

Place the cookies on a baking sheet, and bake the cookies for about seventeen minutes. Make sure you don't brown them!

Cool the cookies. Then, roll each of them in the confectioners' sugar. Enjoy!

Italian Afternoon Rice Pie

Recipe Makes 6 Servings.

Nutritional Information Per Serving: 110 calories, 10 grams carbohydrates, 5 grams fat, 4 grams protein.

Ingredients:

9 eggs

2 cups heavy whipping cream

1 ¾ cups white sugar

1 cup white rice, cooked

2 ½ pounds ricotta cheese

1 tsp. vanilla

15 ounces crushed pineapple

Directions:

Preheat the oven to 325 degrees Fahrenheit.

Beat the eggs together in a large mixing bowl. Add the sugar and continue to mix well.

Next, add the vanilla and the ricotta cheese. The mixture should be smooth and creamy.

Add the heavy cream at this time and continue to stir.

When it's mixed in, add the crushed pineapple and the rice delicately, folding it into the mixture.

Pour the batter into a 9x13 baking pan.

Bake the cake for sixty minutes. Insert a knife into the center of the pie. If it comes out clean, the cake is done.

Refrigerate the pie until it's cooled, and serve.

Enjoy!

Italian Cassata Delight

Recipe Makes 8 Servings.

Nutritional Information Per Serving: 460 calories, 43 grams carbohydrates, 29 grams fat, 8 grams protein.

Ingredients:

½ cup dried currants

3 tbsp. heavy cream

1/3 cup Marsala wine

16 ounces dark cherries

1 pint ricotta cheese

1/3 cup white sugar

1 pound cake package, prepared

1 ounce chopped semisweet chocolate

1 cup butter

Directions:

Bring 2 tbsp. of Marsala and the dried currants together in a small bowl. Allow the currants to soak for twenty minutes before draining and slicing them into fourths or eights.

To the side, puree the ricotta, the sugar, 3 tbsp. of Marsala, and the whipping cream together in the food processor. The mixture should be smooth.

Transfer the mixture into a medium-sized bowl. Add the currants and the cherries.

After you've prepared the pound cake, slice it lengthwise into three layers. Position the very bottom layer on a plate. Spread about half of the filling over the first layer.

Next, place the second layer of the cake over the filling. Spread the rest of the filling over.

Place the final pound cake piece on top. Refrigerate this for two hours.

Next, create the chocolate frosting by combining the rest of the cherry syrup, the chocolate, and the remaining Marsala in a saucepan.

Stir the mixture over low heat. The chocolate should melt and become smooth.

Remove the heat and add the butter. Whisk while it melts.

Refrigerate this frosting for twenty minutes, stirring every few minutes.

Bring the frosting into a pastry bag. Spread the chocolate frosting over the cake utilizing the pastry bag and pipe.

Refrigerate the cake until completely set. Slice the cake, serve, and enjoy!

ITALIAN TIRAMISU

Recipe Makes 12 Servings.

Nutritional Information Per Serving: 420 calories, 42 grams carbohydrates, 28 grams fat, 4 grams protein.

Ingredients:

11 ounces frozen and pre-prepared pound cake. Sliced into 9 pieces.

1 cup coffee, brewed

1 cup sugar

8 ounces cream cheese

¾ cup chocolate syrup

2 cups heavy whipping cream

3 ounces English toffee with chocolate coating, diced

Directions:

Place the pieces of pound cake at the bottom of a 9x13 pan. Pour the coffee over the cake, making sure to hit every piece of it.

Stir together the chocolate syrup, the sugar, and the cream cheese in a large mixing bowl. Add the whipping cream and stir until fluffy.

Spread the mixture over the cake. Then, sprinkle the cake with the toffee candies.

Cover the cake and allow it to chill for sixty minutes.

Serve the cake cold, and enjoy!

Conclusion:

The Italian Healthy Recipes Cookbook offers stunning, vibrant, and nutritious foods for your appetizer, salad, soup, pizza, pasta, and dessert needs.

Truly, you can assimilate into the Italian lifestyle. You can laze about, eating olives, feeling the ingredients as they take hold of you and make you happier and healthier than you've ever been.

Whether you want to impress your friends with a full-course meal or simply enjoy a beautiful pizza at home with your loved one, this book has you covered.

And remember: when you eat Italian, you can expect:

1. Fresh, simplistic ingredients that work to refute your risk of certain diseases, like cancers.
2. Herbs that have healing properties, things like basil, oregano, and parsley.
3. Protein that helps you grow strong muscles and revs your metabolism.
4. Vegetables that enrich your very being.
5. And pasta, of course, that gives you energy—enough energy to live well, to exercise, and to laugh, so much like an Italian.

Enjoy your new Italian lifestyle with these wonderful recipes. Don't turn back from this road of bountiful food and beautiful nutrition.

About The Author

Since Paolo Ferrari moved to the USA from Italy, he was 16 years old, he knew he wanted to be a chef. Growing up, he was incredibly intrigued by cooking and by how he could make people happy through food, so he read as many cook books as he could get his hands on, and took as many cooking courses as possible.

When he was still attending high school, Paolo began working at a steakhouse. He has remained a member of the team since then, only leaving long enough to earn a degree in culinary arts from The Florida Culinary Institute in Palm Beach, FL in 2010.

Paolo is now a paleo lifestyle expert on his own time. He is passionate about the diet and believes everyone should give it a shot.

OTHER BOOKS BY CHEF PAOLO

PALEO SALAD RECIPES: 45 EASY-TO-PREPARE, DELICIOUS, HEALTHY, AND PALEO SALAD RECIPES

PALEO CHICKEN RECIPES: 45 STEP-BY-STEP, EASY TO MAKE, HEALTHY CHICKEN RECIPES

ULTIMATE GUIDE TO THE PALEO DIET: PALEO DIET FOR BEGINNERS: PALEO FOR BEGINNERS

ONE LAST THING...

If you enjoyed this book or found it useful I'd be very grateful if you'd post a short review on Amazon. Your support really does make a difference and I read all the reviews personally so I can get your feedback and make this book even better.

Thanks again for your support!

Printed in Poland
by Amazon Fulfillment
Poland Sp. z o.o., Wrocław

51005454R00038